VOLCANOES

Anna Claybourne

KINGFISHER

BOSTON

KINGFISHER

a Houghton Mifflin Company imprint
222 Berkeley Street
Boston, Massachusetts 02116
www.houghtonmifflinbooks.com

First published in 2007
10 9 8 7 6 5 4 3 2 1
1TR/0507/GCUP/UNITED(UNITED)/140MA/F

LIBRARY OF CONGRESS CATALOGING-IN-PUBLICATION DATA
has been applied for.

ISBN 978-0-7534-6137-2

For Q2A Media
Editor: Honor Head
Consultant: Terry Jennings
Designer: Chaya Sajwan
Art director: Rahul Dhiman
Illustrators: Rishi Bhardwaj, Amit Tayal. Aadil A. Siddiqui,
    and Subhash C. Vohra
Image researcher: Jyoti Sachdev

For Kingfisher
Editorial manager: Russell McLean
Coordinating editor: Caitlin Doyle
Art director: Mike Davis
DTP manager: Nicky Studdart
DTP operator: Claire Cessford
Senior production controller: Lindsey Scott

Printed in China

NOTE TO READERS
The website addresses listed in this book are correct at the time
of going to print. However, due to the ever-changing nature of the
Internet, website addresses and content can change. Websites can
contain links that are unsuitable for children. The publisher cannot
be held responsible for changes in website addresses or content or
for information obtained through third-party websites. We strongly
advise that Internet searches are supervised by an adult.

CONTENTS

Kilauea
The most active volcano in the world is Kilauea on the island of Hawaii.

Surtsey
In 1963 the volcanic island of Surtsey appeared out of the sea near Iceland.

Surtsey
Iceland

NORTH AMERICA

PACIFIC OCEAN

Saint Helens
Washington

Kilauea
Hawaii

Paricutin
Mexico

ATLANTIC OCEAN

Arenal
Costa Rica

Pelée
Martinique, West Indies

Nevado del Ruiz
Colombia

SOUTH AMERICA

WORLD OF VOLCANOES

At any given time, at least 20 active volcanoes are erupting around the world. Right now hot, molten rock from deep inside Earth is bursting out of the ground. It breaks up into choking black volcanic ash that fills the air or flows down the mountain slopes, burning trees, crops, and even animals and people.

Deadly disasters

As well as showering its surroundings with seething lava at a temperature of more than 1,832°F (1,000°C)—ten times hotter than boiling water—an exploding volcano flings out rocks, ash, mud, and poisonous gases. Volcanoes have caused many of the most famous and deadly natural disasters in Earth's history.

Rich growth

Volcanoes are not all bad news. Volcanic eruptions build new mountains and create land out of the ocean. Many rocks and minerals formed inside volcanoes are useful and valuable to us. Throughout the ages, people who live near volcanoes have found that the soil is excellent for growing crops because of the mineral-rich ash that falls onto it.

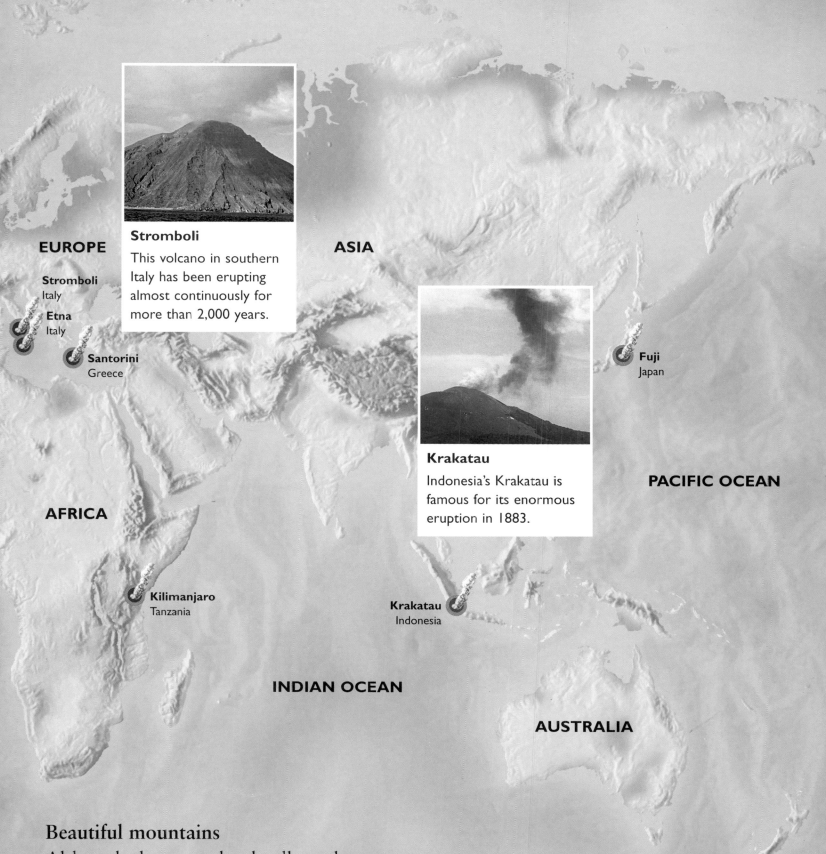

EUROPE

ASIA

Stromboli
Italy

Etna
Italy

Santorini
Greece

Stromboli
This volcano in southern Italy has been erupting almost continuously for more than 2,000 years.

Fuji
Japan

Krakatau
Indonesia's Krakatau is famous for its enormous eruption in 1883.

PACIFIC OCEAN

AFRICA

Kilimanjaro
Tanzania

Krakatau
Indonesia

INDIAN OCEAN

AUSTRALIA

Beautiful mountains

Although they may be deadly, volcanoes can also be stunningly beautiful. Some of them, such as snow-covered Mount Fuji in Japan and cloud-capped Mount Kilimanjaro in Tanzania, have long been thought of as sacred sites and are loved as much as they are feared.

All around the world
There are volcanoes on every continent. This map shows some of the world's best known and most active volcanoes. "Active" means that a volcano is erupting or has erupted recently.

ANTARCTICA

Eruption!

Some volcanoes erupt slowly. Their lava seeps to the surface in a constant, gentle flow. But the classic volcanic eruption is a sudden, violent explosion. Before such an eruption happens, magma—molten rock from inside Earth—pushes upward and collects underneath the volcano. Once it leaves the volcano, magma is called lava.

Under pressure

As the pressure of the magma builds up underneath, lava may begin to leak out of the sides of the volcano, which can start to bulge and shake. These signs warn that it is about to erupt. When the volcano finally blows its top, hot lava, ash, rocks, gases, and dust burst out with an enormous roar.

Ash cloud

As lava comes to the surface, it can cool, harden, and shatter, forming volcanic ash. A powerful eruption can throw burning hot ash, mixed with dust, gas, and mud, several miles into the air.

River of fire

Boiling hot liquid lava flows down the sides of the volcano, forming lava rivers and pools. Because it is thick and sticky, it usually flows slowly.

Hurling rocks

When a volcano erupts, a huge amount of energy is released. As the pressurized magma and gas suddenly escape and expand, ash, dust, and chunks of solid rock are hurled high up into the sky. An eruption releases vast amounts of heat, too.

Incredible energy

The eruption of Krakatau in 1883 is thought to have released 200 megatons of energy—the equivalent of 15,000 nuclear bombs. Volcanic energy also takes the form of sound. The explosion of Krakatau made a boom that could be heard on the island of Rodrigues, around 3,000 mi. (4,800km) away. Volcanoes are too dangerous and unpredictable for us to be able to harness most of their energy.

Rocks, bombs, and blocks

As a volcano erupts, it blows up solid rocks from the outside of the mountain, forcing pebbles and boulders into the air. Lava can also cool and harden as it flies through the air, forming solid lumps known as volcanic bombs or blocks.

The aftermath

A big volcanic eruption can go on for hours, days, or weeks. Afterward the countryside, towns, and villages nearby may be unrecognizable. Sometimes a layer of ash and dust settles onto the landscape, choking plants and animals, blocking roads, and ruining homes.

Path of destruction

Flows of lava and hot ash burn everything in their path to cinders, reducing forests, prairies, and fields of crops to blackened wasteland. It can take many years for an area devastated by a volcanic eruption to recover fully.

Mudflow mayhem

Mud can be a deadly result of an eruption. Sometimes mudflows engulf towns and drown thousands of people.

Death and disaster

Although volcanic eruptions are loud, fiery, and violent, the actual eruption itself rarely kills many people. This is because the center of the eruption is usually at the top of a mountain, away from settlements, and there is usually some warning.

Choking and suffocating

Yet the results of a volcanic eruption can cause mass destruction. Fine ash falling onto a town or village can choke and suffocate people and animals. Volcanic landslides and mudflows may flatten villages and farms. Big volcanic eruptions can also send shock waves into the sea, creating lethal tsunamis. And if a volcano wipes out crops and livestock, the local people may suffer a deadly famine.

Coated in ash

In 1991 the eruption of Mount Pinatubo in the Philippines left a layer of ash 6.5 ft. (2m) deep over a radius of 2 mi. (3km) around the volcano. Farther away, streets and cars were covered in enough ash to make travel impossible.

Flattened by the blast

Hot lava and ash, flying rocks, and landslides can leave a forest burned, blackened, and barren following a volcanic eruption.

EXPLODING EARTH

In March 1980, Mount Saint Helens, a beautiful snowcapped volcano in the United States, suddenly started to tremble. Slowly, its north side began to bulge outward as it prepared to erupt. Finally, at 8:32 A.M. on May 18, the volcano blew up with an earsplitting boom. It was a spectacular eruption, but why did it happen?

Underground studies

Volcanoes are difficult to study. They are dangerous, and the events that make the explosions happen occur deep underground. But scientists have discovered a lot about how volcanoes work and why they come in so many different sizes, shapes, and styles.

Rivers of rock

Pyroclastic flows can surge forward at speeds of up to 150 mph (240km/h). It is impossible to outrun them or drive away from them. Searing heat, poisonous gases, and choking dust make them deadly for any living thing caught in their path.

Blowing apart

When the crust of rock covering the north side of Mount Saint Helens fell away, a high-pressure mixture of hot magma (molten rock), ash, and superheated steam inside was released and burst outward. Some of the material rose into the air in vast clouds, while the rest formed rivers of hot ash, small rocks, and gases known as pyroclastic flows.

Death and destruction

The deadly rivers thundered down the volcano's steep slopes, obliterating everything in their path. The area had been evacuated, but 57 people were killed, including a volcanologist (volcano scientist), David Johnston, who had gone to observe the volcano. The eruption also killed thousands of deer and elk and destroyed roads, railroads, homes, and farmland.

Changing shape

The 1980 eruption of Mount Saint Helens lasted for more than nine hours and blew away a huge chunk of the mountain. These pictures show its shape before the explosion (top) and afterward (above).

Inside a volcano

Bombs

Blocks

Most volcanoes are mountains. This is because as a volcano erupts, lava, ash, and rocks pile up and cool all around it, building it higher and higher. Unlike a normal mountain, which is just a mound of rocks, a volcano has a channel, called a vent, that leads right inside Earth. When a volcano is dormant (sleeping) or when an active volcano is not erupting, the top of the vent may be blocked with cooled, hardened lava. But underneath, hot magma is collecting, ready for the next eruption.

Bombs and blocks

Bombs and blocks are big pieces of rocks and lava that are thrown out of a volcano. Blocks are solid chunks of rock and can be as big as a bus. Bombs are smaller and made of semimolten lava. They often form a teardrop shape as they fly through the air.

Active craters

The crater of a volcano, such as this one in Vanuatu in the Pacific Ocean, usually looks like a huge, gaping, bowl-shaped hollow. Steam and gas may pour from the crater, even when the volcano is not erupting.

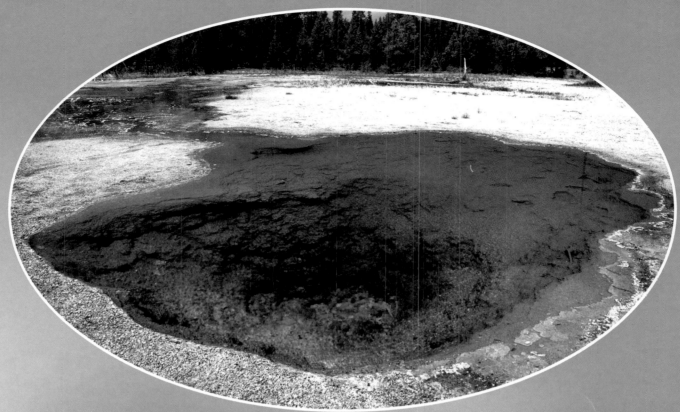

Volcanic water features

The hot underground magma in volcanic areas often heats up water under the ground. The heated water rises to the surface in the form of a hot spring (above), a jet of steam, called a fumarole, or a hot fountain, called a geyser.

The parts of a volcano

In the ground underneath a volcano is a magma chamber—a huge mass of hot, melted rock. The magma pushes toward the surface up a tube called a pipe. This leads into the vent, which travels up the center of the volcano. The top of the vent opens out into the crater, where lava flows out of the volcano. It may also flow out through smaller side vents called dikes. The volcano's flanks (slopes) are made up of layers of old, cooled lava from previous eruptions.

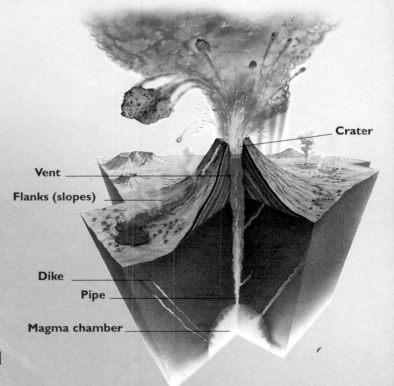

Crater

Vent

Flanks (slopes)

Dike

Pipe

Magma chamber

Red-hot lava

When molten rock is inside Earth, it is called magma. Once it emerges through Earth's surface during a volcanic eruption, it is known as lava. Most of the rock just under Earth's surface is not molten magma, but harder, more solid rock. The magma is found only in certain parts of Earth. It moves up through a weakness in Earth's crust and forces its way to the surface, forming volcanoes.

Types of lavas

There are several different types of lavas, depending on the types of rocks from which they are made. For example, felsic lavas contain the minerals quartz and feldspar and are thick and sticky, while mafic lavas contain basalt rocks and are thin and runny. Scientists have found that the type of lava in a volcano plays a large part in the way that it erupts.

Slow or sudden?

If the lava is very thick and sticky, it cannot flow fast. Gases get trapped inside, and it builds up in a high-pressure mass before exploding. In a Plinian-type eruption, the volcano explodes, turning the thick lava to ash. In a Strombolian-type eruption, big lumps of thick, sticky lava fly out of the volcano. Thin, runny lava leads to gentler Hawaiian-type eruptions. The lava forms fountains, puddles, and streams as it flows smoothly from the volcano.

Cooling and hardening

As lava cools, it hardens into different types of rock formations. Pahoehoe is a type of rock that looks like strands of rope and is formed by smooth, runny lava. Aa is rough, craggy volcanic rock made by a lava flow cracking and folding over as it hardens. Pillow lava (right) forms when lava cools underwater. As each plume of hot lava is released, it hardens into a bubble-shaped "pillow."

Strombolian

In a Strombolian-type eruption, clots, or lumps, of semimolten lava fly upward out of the volcano and land all around it. Yasur, a volcano on Vanuatu, a Pacific island, is famous for its Strombolian eruptions.

Plinian

In a Plinian-type eruption, pressure builds up in thick, viscous lava until it explodes out of the volcano in a cloud of ash and dust that rises high up into the stratosphere.

Hawaiian

In a Hawaiian-type eruption, smooth, runny lava spurts, runs, and flows out of a volcano.

15

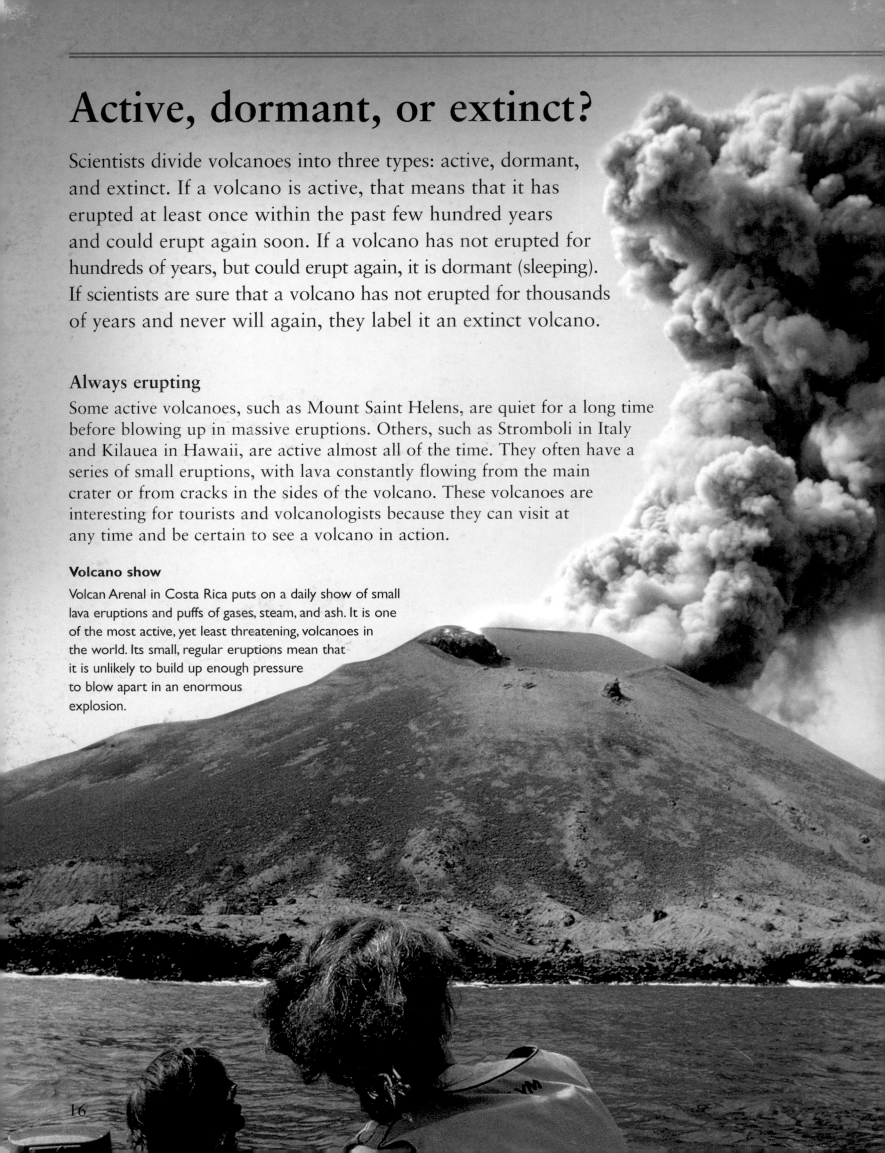

Active, dormant, or extinct?

Scientists divide volcanoes into three types: active, dormant, and extinct. If a volcano is active, that means that it has erupted at least once within the past few hundred years and could erupt again soon. If a volcano has not erupted for hundreds of years, but could erupt again, it is dormant (sleeping). If scientists are sure that a volcano has not erupted for thousands of years and never will again, they label it an extinct volcano.

Always erupting

Some active volcanoes, such as Mount Saint Helens, are quiet for a long time before blowing up in massive eruptions. Others, such as Stromboli in Italy and Kilauea in Hawaii, are active almost all of the time. They often have a series of small eruptions, with lava constantly flowing from the main crater or from cracks in the sides of the volcano. These volcanoes are interesting for tourists and volcanologists because they can visit at any time and be certain to see a volcano in action.

Volcano show

Volcan Arenal in Costa Rica puts on a daily show of small lava eruptions and puffs of gases, steam, and ash. It is one of the most active, yet least threatening, volcanoes in the world. Its small, regular eruptions mean that it is unlikely to build up enough pressure to blow apart in an enormous explosion.

Kilauea's crater

Although Kilauea in Hawaii is probably the world's most active volcano, you can walk right up to the edge of its crater. Its most recent eruption, called the Pu'u 'O'o eruption, has been going on continuously since 1983.

Deceptively dormant

It can be very hard to tell the difference between a dormant volcano and an extinct volcano. Most people thought that Mount Vesuvius, a famous volcano in Italy, was extinct before it blew up in A.D. 79, killing around 3,500 people.

Volcano shapes

On Hawaii Island stands the world's largest active volcano, Mauna Loa. But Mauna Loa is not a huge, pointed cone; it is a massive, flattened hump, 75 mi. (120km) long and 64 mi. (103km) wide. Mauna Loa is a shield volcano—named this because it resembles a huge, curved shield lying on the ground. The shape of a volcano is determined by the way that it erupts and the type of lava that flows from it. The three main volcano shapes are shield, cinder cone, and stratovolcano.

Shaped by lava

Volcanoes are built by the lava, ash, and rocks that come out of them. If the lava is thin and runny, it flows gently out of the volcano, as in Hawaiian-type eruptions, running a long way before it cools and hardens. It spreads out over a wide area, creating a broad, gently sloping shield volcano. Strombolian-type eruptions throw out many small lumps of lava, which build up to form a steep-sided cone shape with a wide crater—a cinder cone volcano. Stratovolcanoes can erupt suddenly after a long silence, with a Plinian-type eruption of thick, sticky lava. Lava, ash, and rocks build up around the crater, making a sharply pointed volcano with slightly curving sides.

Shield volcano
Runny lava spreads out as it flows gently from the volcano, forming a low, flat mound.

Tall and pointed

Mount Fuji in Japan is a stratovolcano made up of layers of cooled lava, ash, and debris deposited by ash falls and pyroclastic flows.

Cinder cone volcano

Repeated small, violent eruptions blast a wide crater and build up layers of lava and cinders into a cone shape. Of the three main shapes, cinder cones are the smallest and most common.

Stratovolcano

Large, explosive eruptions of sticky lava build up a pointed spout around the crater. The mountain is formed from layers of ash, rocks, and lava.

Shallow slopes

The wide, dark hill of Mauna Loa looms over Hawaii Island. As well as being the world's largest active volcano, Mauna Loa is also the world's biggest (though not the highest) mountain. It has erupted more than 30 times since its recorded activity began in 1843.

How a caldera is made

Sometimes a volcano erupts so violently that a huge chunk of the mountain is blown away (1), leaving a ring-shaped hollow called a caldera (2). The caldera often fills up with water, making a crater lake (3).

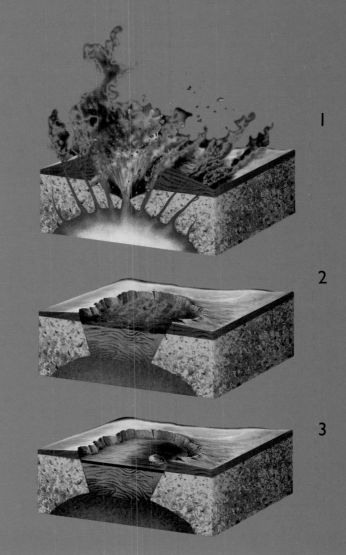

1

2

3

Santorini

The Greek island of Santorini is an island caldera left behind by the eruption of a huge volcano in around 1630 B.C.

FAMOUS ERUPTIONS

On August 27, 1883, the island volcano of
Krakatau, Indonesia, blew itself to pieces. The huge
explosion was one of the biggest volcanic eruptions
in history. Even though the island was uninhabited,
the eruption claimed the lives of at least 36,000
people as a result of the showers of burning ash
and the huge tsunamis that it caused.

Before and after
The 1883 eruption completely changed the
shape of Krakatau island. The top picture
shows it before the eruption, and the
bottom picture shows it after the eruption.

Krakatau explodes
The 1883 eruption of Krakatau was not caught on camera
because photography was still in its early stages. However,
many people witnessed it, and the explosion was recorded
in the form of paintings, engravings, and woodcuts.

Killer Krakatau

How did Krakatau kill so many people? First, the explosion hurled burning rocks and volcanic ash high up into the air, which wiped out thousands of people—for example, all 3,000 inhabitants on the nearby island of Sebesi were killed. Next, as the volcano blew apart, its north side collapsed into the ocean, creating a giant tsunami. The tsunami waves spread out across the Indian Ocean, reaching 130 ft. (40m) high near some coasts. They devastated coastal towns and villages and overturned boats, which killed thousands more people.

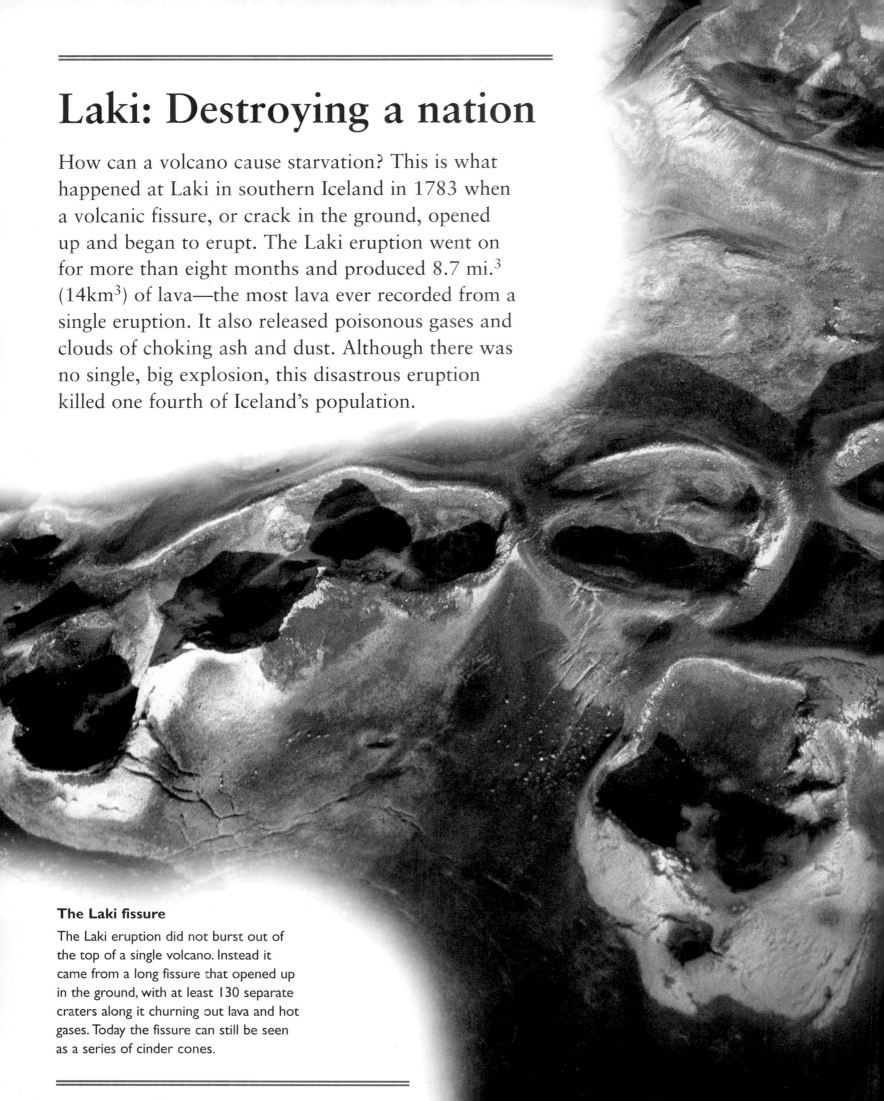

Laki: Destroying a nation

How can a volcano cause starvation? This is what happened at Laki in southern Iceland in 1783 when a volcanic fissure, or crack in the ground, opened up and began to erupt. The Laki eruption went on for more than eight months and produced 8.7 mi.^{3} (14km^3) of lava—the most lava ever recorded from a single eruption. It also released poisonous gases and clouds of choking ash and dust. Although there was no single, big explosion, this disastrous eruption killed one fourth of Iceland's population.

The Laki fissure

The Laki eruption did not burst out of the top of a single volcano. Instead it came from a long fissure that opened up in the ground, with at least 130 separate craters along it churning out lava and hot gases. Today the fissure can still be seen as a series of cinder cones.

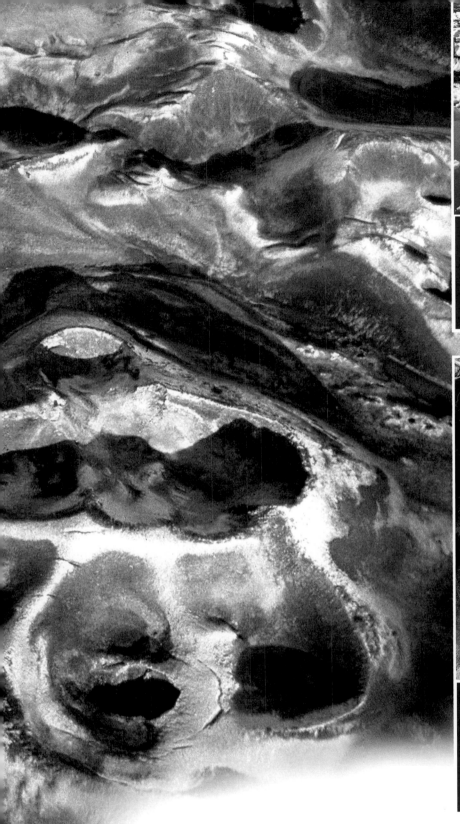

Freezing winters

The Laki eruption released so much gas into the atmosphere that it affected the climate, making the winter of 1783–1784 unusually cold across North America and northern Europe.

Divided island

This map shows how Iceland is split by the Mid-Atlantic Ridge, shown in yellow. The Mid-Atlantic Ridge is a boundary between two of the huge tectonic plates (see page 33) that make up Earth's crust. There is a lot of activity where the plates meet.

Suffocating and starving

Hundreds of people died in the Laki eruption as a result of lava flows, choking dust, poisonous gases, and floods caused by melting ice. But worse was to come. One of the volcanic gases spewed out by the eruption was fluorine. It seeped across the countryside and was absorbed into the grass and other plants. When farm animals ate the grass, they were poisoned and died. More than three fourths of Iceland's cattle and sheep—200,000 animals—were killed, leading to a famine that wiped out 9,000 people. Records show that death rates peaked in other northern countries too, so pollution from the eruption probably claimed thousands more lives elsewhere.

Ruiz: Rivers of mud

Nevado del Ruiz, a volcano in Colombia, has unleashed deadly lahars, or mudflows, onto the surrounding villages three times. In the first eruption, in 1595, 600 people died. In the second, in 1845, more than 1,000 people were killed. Then, on November 13, 1985, the volcano erupted again. When a rain of ash and dust fell on the town of Armero, 46 mi. (74km) from the summit, the people wondered if they should evacuate—but the ash fall stopped, and so they stayed. Then at 11 P.M. that night, a rushing, roaring wall of mud, laden with rocks and boulders, descended on the town, smashing its buildings and drowning 23,000 of its inhabitants.

Armero: The aftermath

The day after the 1985 eruption of Nevado del Ruiz, this was all that remained of the town of Armero. It had been built on top of the old, hardened mudflow from Ruiz's previous major eruption in 1845. The 1985 mudflow took exactly the same path, drowning most of the town.

Rainstorm eruptions

Volcanic lahars happen when boiling lava, or a pyroclastic flow of hot rocks and ash, combines with water to create a hot, fast-moving river of mud. Lahars can result from a volcanic eruption during a heavy rainstorm. More often, as in the case of Nevado del Ruiz, the hot lava and ash melt the volcano's cap of snow and ice, creating a torrent of water.

Fast-flowing danger

The mud in a lahar is runny, not thick and sticky. It surges down the mountain's river valleys at speeds of up to 62 mph (100km/h)—and the lahar may be so big that it can engulf a medium-size town, such as Armero, in a few minutes. Even so, Armero's residents could have escaped by walking less than one mile to higher ground if they had known that the mud was coming. Modern satellite-warning systems would probably be able to prevent a disaster like this one from happening again by giving the local people enough warning time to flee.

Nevado del Ruiz
Nevado del Ruiz, a stratovolcano, is Colombia's highest active volcano at 17,680 ft. (5,389m) high. The disastrous eruption of 1985 was its most recent, but it could erupt again.

Helping survivors
A rescuer helps a survivor of the 1985 Nevado del Ruiz disaster.

Pompeii: Entombed in ash

If you visit the remains of Pompeii near Naples, Italy, you will see a Roman city preserved in every detail. Streets, houses, stores, theaters, wall paintings, and everyday objects were frozen in time when the nearby volcano Vesuvius erupted in A.D. 79. After the first eruption threw a column of ash into the sky, pyroclastic flows engulfed the city in a layer of hot ash and dust up to 3 ft. (7m) deep. Anyone who had not left when the volcano began to rumble and the first rocks and ash fell was killed instantly by the deadly, choking dust.

Violent Vesuvius

The eruption of Vesuvius was violent and powerful—it was a Plinian-type eruption. These eruptions get their name from the philosopher Pliny's description of Vesuvius.

Body casts

When pyroclastic flows burst into Pompeii, everything was covered with ash, which later cooled and solidified. The bodies of the victims caught in the ash eventually rotted away, leaving empty hollows. Plaster casts made from these hollows reveal the shapes of the people and animals in their dying moments.

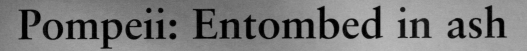

According to Pliny

The remains of Pompeii tell their own story, but we also have a written account of the eruption by the Roman philosopher Pliny the Younger. When Vesuvius began to erupt on August 24, Pliny was staying with his uncle, Pliny the Elder, in Misenum, across the bay from Pompeii.

Crying out

When they saw the volcano begin to erupt, Pliny the Elder set off by boat to observe the eruption and rescue friends. He landed in Stabiae, near Pompeii, and found his friend Pomponianus, but they could not escape. Pliny the Elder died, along with more than 2,000 of Pompeii's residents. Pliny the Younger escaped. He wrote: "You could hear the shrieks of women, the wailing of infants, and the shouting of men; some were calling their parents, others their children or their wives."

Uncovering Pompeii

For hundreds of years, Pompeii lay buried beneath its layer of ash, and vineyards were planted on top. In 1594 workers digging a new canal discovered some of the ruins, but it was not until the 1700s that archaeologists began to excavate the whole city. Today, Pompeii is a huge tourist attraction.

27

Mount Pelée: Deadly gases

In late April 1902, Mount Pelée, on the French Caribbean island of Martinique, began to erupt. Saint Pierre, the prosperous town on the coast below the volcano, was showered with ash and enveloped in a smelly cloud of sulfur. Then poisonous snakes and insects invaded the city, driven away from the mountainside by the earthquakes and ash falls. Dozens of people died from snakebites.

Deadly mistake

When a lahar killed 23 workers in a factory north of the city on May 5, people began to talk about escaping to another town on the island, Forte de France. But the governor declared the volcano and Saint Pierre to be safe. In fact, many people from surrounding villages crowded into the city, convinced that it was the safest place to be. They were very, very wrong.

Powerful Pelée

The blast of hot gases, rocks, and ash was so forceful that it knocked down all of the walls in its path. It even toppled a three-ton statue and carried it 52 ft. (16m) away. Most of the people, if they were not crushed by the falling buildings, were killed by the intense heat of the burning gases.

The gases strike

The townspeople of Saint Pierre tried to continue with their lives, but on May 8 at 7:50 P.M., Mount Pelée erupted again, this time with more force than ever. A terrifying pyroclastic flow of red-hot, glowing gases, ash, and stones rolled down the mountain at 62 mph (100km/h), directly onto Saint Pierre. Almost the entire population of 20,000, plus an extra 8,000 people who had come to the city for safety, were suffocated and burned alive by the deadly gases.

A few survivors

Sailors on ships moored in the harbor stared in horror as the city was destroyed, just before the ball of gas spread out across the water and enveloped the boats, too. On land only two people survived. One was a prisoner, Louis-Auguste Cyparis. He was being held in the city dungeon and survived because the tiny grate connecting his cell to the outside world let in only a little of the hot gas—enough to burn him, but not to kill him.

A narrow escape
Louis-Auguste Cyparis survived the eruption. He was pardoned and became a circus showman.

Gas cloud in Cameroon
In 1986 Cameroon's Lake Nyos, a lake in the middle of a volcanic crater, released a cloud of around one cubic mile of suffocating carbon dioxide gas. Since carbon dioxide is heavier than air, it rolled downhill and over the village of Lower Nyos, killing hundreds of people and animals.

CHANGING LANDSCAPES

One day in 1943, as Mexican farmer Dionisio Pulido worked in his cornfield, he saw the flat ground heave, swell, and crack open before his eyes. Smoke, ash, and then lava began to erupt from the hole as Pulido ran for his life. What he had seen was the birth of a brand-new volcano, Paricutin.

Something from nothing

Volcanoes are creators as well as destroyers. They can build new land and reshape Earth's surface, form new rocks, and renew the soil. And they work fast—all of this can happen in minutes, hours, or days, instead of the thousands of years it takes for mountains and rocks to be shaped by glaciers, wind, and water erosion.

Swamped steeple

Lava and ash from the birth of Paricutin covered the nearby village of San Juan. All that could still be seen was the church, sticking up through a sea of cooled, broken lava.

New landscape

The eruption of Paricutin meant that people could no longer live in the nearby villages because their homes were destroyed. Where the villages once stood there is now a mass of craggy, cooled lava.

Birth and death

Paricutin erupted from 1943 to 1952. Over the first 24 hours, the eruption created a 164-ft. (50-m) cinder cone, as high as a 16-story apartment building. Paricutin was especially exciting for volcanologists. For the first time it allowed them to watch a volcano being born, growing, and eventually becoming extinct—they were able to witness the entire life cycle of a volcano.

Tourists gaze at the spectacle of Paricutin erupting.

This chart shows how Paricutin grew over its nine-year eruption, from 1943 to 1952. It grew fast to begin with, and then it gradually slowed down.

Growth of a volcano

1 day	64 ft. (50m)
1 week	328 ft. (100m)
1 year	1,102 ft. (336m)
9 years (final height)	1,391 ft. (424m)

Shaping Earth

Millions of years of volcanic eruptions have shaped a lot of Earth's landscapes. Even in places where there are no active volcanoes, you can see mountains and hills that are the remains of old volcanoes. When a volcano erupts, it can change the horizon overnight by adding to its own height or blowing itself apart. And in the oceans, constant volcanic eruptions create a new seabed.

Jigsaw-puzzle Earth

Earth is covered with a rocky, solid crust floating on top of hot, molten, and semimolten magma. This crust is divided into several huge pieces, like the pieces of a jigsaw puzzle, called tectonic plates. The plates are constantly moving because of volcanic activity around their plate boundaries, or edges. There are two main types of plate boundaries. At spreading ridges, magma pushes out from inside Earth and forms new crust. As it spreads out, it pushes apart the plates. At subduction zones, one plate plunges underneath another one deep in the Earth, where it melts and forms new magma.

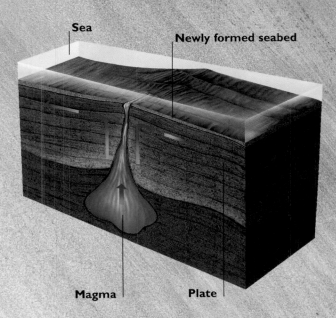

Sea　　Newly formed seabed

Magma　　Plate

Spreading ridge

At a spreading ridge, two plates are pushed apart as magma rises out of Earth's crust and hardens.

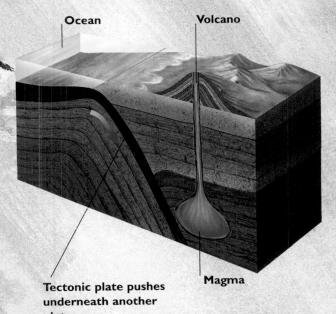

Ocean　　Volcano

Tectonic plate pushes underneath another plate

Magma

Subduction zone

At a subduction zone, one plate pushes beneath another one and melts into new magma. Volcanoes are most common along the tectonic plate boundaries on land and in the ocean.

Fiery beginnings

Billions of years ago, when Earth was newly formed, volcanoes were more common than they are now. Huge volcanic eruptions created many of the mountains and landscapes that we can see today.

Treasure troves

When 15-year-old Erasmus Jacobs found a strange white rock on his father's farm one day in 1866, he had no idea that his discovery would make his country, South Africa, rich. What he had found was a huge diamond, carried out of Earth by a volcano.

Rock factories

Volcanoes create rocks and minerals in two main ways. The magma and lava in a volcano is made of molten rock. It cools and hardens into different types of rocks—such as hard, black basalt; light, rough-textured pumice; and tough, grainy granite. These types of rocks, formed from lava, are called igneous (meaning "fiery") rocks.

Rocky pinnacles

These rock formations sticking up out of the ground at the Pinnacles National Monument in California were created by an ancient volcano.

Changing rocks

Volcanoes can also change existing rocks by subjecting them to high heat and pressure. For example, limestone rock in the ground near a volcanic vent can change into a different rock, marble, if it is heated and squeezed by hot underground magma. Rocks created in this way are called metamorphic rocks.

Underground search

Miners make their way through a tunnel in a diamond mine near Pretoria, South Africa, searching for diamonds trapped in the rocks.

Earth's riches

Diamonds are formed in magma beneath Earth's crust and get trapped in rocks that are created when volcanoes erupt—such as kimberlite. Volcanoes give us not only diamonds but also many precious stones, such as obsidian and peridot, and useful rocks and minerals. Pumice is a rock made from lava that contains bubbles of gas. When the lava cools, the bubbles are trapped inside the rock, making pumice very light. Because of its texture, pumice has been used for thousands of years to exfoliate (rub away) rough skin.

Black sand beach

Some volcanic islands, such as Hawaii and Iceland, have black beaches. They are made from basalt—an igneous rock formed when lava cools—that has been broken down into sand particles by the action of waves.

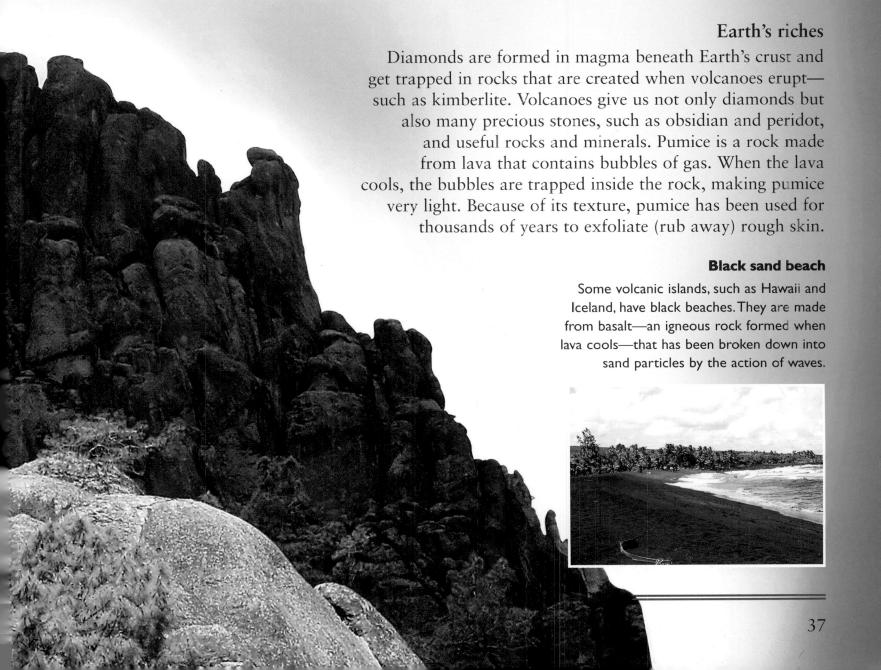

Starting again

When a big volcano erupts, it can change the land around it for years to come. A thick covering of dust and ash swamps plant life and chokes the soil. Pyroclastic flows destroy even the biggest trees, and a layer of cooled, hardened lava covers the land in bare rocks. The empty, barren wasteland can take decades to return to normal.

Fertile farming

Highly volcanic areas have some of the most fertile farmland in the world. This crop of rice is growing in Bali, Indonesia, in the shadow of a volcano.

Coming back to life

First, simple plants, such as mosses and lichens, grow from spores carried on the wind. Insects and birds arrive to feed on these plants. Bird droppings, plant matter, and crumbling rock particles then build a layer of soil in which bigger plants and trees can grow. As soil gradually gathers, it collects in folds and cracks in the rocks, and small plants can begin to put down roots. Plant leaves, fruit, and seeds provide food for animals, so once plants are established, more animals can arrive.

Bringing fertility

Volcanic eruptions are often disastrous for farmers. Lava flows, lahars, poisonous gases, or a thick layer of ash can destroy crops, make fields useless, and ruin a lifetime's work. A lighter sprinkling of ash, however, is a different story. Volcanic ash often contains minerals such as potassium and phosphorus, on which plants thrive.

Precious land

Farmland around volcanoes is very fertile. It can grow bumper crops of produce such as onions, citrus fruit, olives, and grapes for winemaking, which are often renowned for their rich flavors. Even a large, damaging eruption will eventually leave the land more fertile. This is one reason why people often choose to live and farm close to active volcanoes, despite the dangers. In 2004 the kingdom of Jordan even gave U.S. President George W. Bush a state gift of six jars of volcanic soil, showing how highly it is valued.

After the eruption

Life slowly returns to the volcanic rocks around a volcano. Lichen grows on the rocks, and soil begins to collect in crevices, allowing grasses and small plants to take hold and thrive.

Soil recipe

Soil is made up of pieces of rock, along with plant and animal matter. After a volcanic eruption, the basic ingredients for soil gradually build up.

VOLCANOES AND PEOPLE

For as long as they have been erupting, volcanoes have been important to the people who live close to them. With their sudden explosions, roaring, booming, and flinging of fire and rocks, it is no surprise that many early peoples thought that volcanoes were mighty gods. Others believed that they were the homes of gods. In Greek mythology, the great god of fire, Hephaestus, used a volcano as a forge to make weapons. In Hawaii, the volcano goddess Pele was said to start volcanic eruptions when she was angry by digging in the ground with a magical stick. Japan's Mount Fuji is the traditional home of the Shinto goddess Konohana Sakuya Hime.

Holy mountain
The volcano Mount Fuji in Japan is sacred to followers of the Shinto religion.

God of fire
The ancient Greeks believed that Hephaestus had a forge under a volcano where he used the fire to make weapons and armor. His Roman name was Vulcan. The word "volcano" comes from Vulcan.

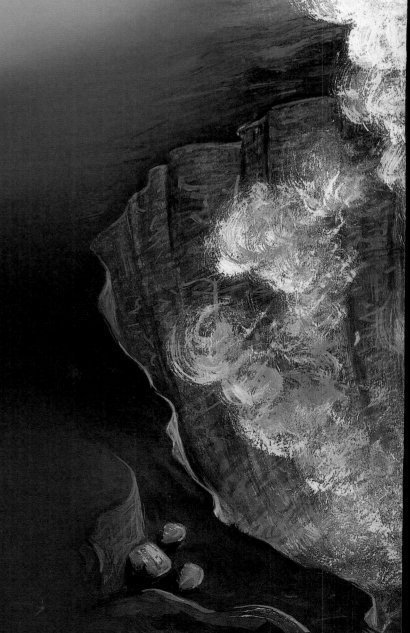

Ancient stories

For thousands of years, humans have created myths and legends as explanations for natural events, and there are many old stories about volcanoes. The ancient Greeks told how Prometheus stole fire from Hephaestus's volcano and gave it to humans. The myth of the lost city of Atlantis sinking beneath the waves may be based on the Greek island of Santorini, which exploded and collapsed into the sea in ancient times. And in the volcanic region of Kamchatka in northeastern Russia, people used to believe that giant demons lived on the tops of volcanoes. At night it was thought that the demons went down to the sea to catch fish and then cooked them—which is why the volcanoes glowed with fire.

Human sacrifices

According to local legends, people used to throw young girls into the fiery crater of the Masaya volcano in Nicaragua. They were hoping to appease the fire goddess Chaciutique so that she would stop the volcano from erupting.

Living with volcanoes

Around the world, more than 300 million people—almost one in 20 of the planet's population—live in the shadows of active volcanoes, where they are at risk from eruptions. Mount Vesuvius in Italy, Mount Rainier in the United States, and Popocatépetl in Mexico are just three volcanoes in highly populated areas that could erupt at any time. So why do people live close to volcanoes? There are two main reasons. First, fertile volcanic soil makes good farmland, which provides a living for millions of people. Second, poverty and overcrowding mean that for many people living close to volcanoes, it is impossible to leave.

After an eruption
When Mount Pinatubo in the Philippines erupted in 1991, many people lost their homes and farms. Around 700 people died in the tragedy, but many more lives were saved. Because scientists were able to predict when the eruption would take place, people had time to leave the danger zone, and the government moved almost 70,000 people to safety.

Being prepared

Scientists are learning more and more about how to predict a volcanic eruption (see page 50), and modern technology, such as satellite imaging, makes it much easier to see what is happening on remote volcanic mountaintops. If an eruption is predicted, the best course of action is to evacuate the area as soon as possible. When a volcano erupts, those left behind might be able to protect themselves by staying inside and avoiding river valleys and low-lying areas where poisonous gases or mudflows could be headed.

Town under fire

Eldfell is a volcano on the Icelandic island of Heimaey. When it erupted in 1973, lava flows threatened to engulf the town of Vestmannaeyjar. The town was evacuated, but some of the islanders stayed to battle with the lava, spraying it with seawater (left) to cool it down and keep it away from the houses. They succeeded in saving a large part of the town, although dozens of homes were lost.

Volcano power

In some volcanic areas, such as Iceland, heat energy from magma under the ground can be used to heat water and run power plants. Water is pumped into the ground, where magma heats it up. The hot water returns to the surface and is used to make steam. The steam is used to power turbines and generate electricity. This type of energy is called "geothermal" (meaning "Earth heat") energy.

On the surface, the heat energy is used to make steam, which drives turbines, generating electricity.

16,400 ft. (5,000m) deep

Cold water moves down

Heated water moves up

Visiting volcanoes

In 1993 a group of scientists and tourists was exploring the crater of the Galeras volcano in Colombia when it suddenly erupted. Six scientists and three tourists were killed. Getting close to volcanoes can be risky, yet we find them fascinating—there are few sights more exciting than a volcano in action. Every day thousands of tourists visit active volcanoes. At many volcano sites you can go right up to the crater. These include Poas in Costa Rica, Kilauea in Hawaii, Bromo in Indonesia, Mutnovsky in Russia, and Vesuvius in Italy. Usually they are very closely checked and monitored and closed to the public at the first signs of a major eruption.

Old Faithful

Old Faithful is a geyser in Yellowstone National Park (Idaho, Montana, and Wyoming). This natural hot water fountain is caused by magma heating underground water. As the water gets hotter, steam builds up under pressure and eventually forces a jet of water out of the ground. Old Faithful goes off every 60–90 minutes for around three minutes at a time.

Hot-spring spas

Hot springs often occur close to volcanoes, where water heated by underground magma flows out of the ground. The water often contains dissolved volcanic minerals that are thought to be good for the skin. This is the Blue Lagoon, a hot-spring spa in Iceland.

Safe to see

Volcanic areas often contain amazing water features, such as geysers, bubbling mud pools, and mineral lakes, which tourists can visit safely. Some have volcanic spas where naturally hot, volcanic springs are deliberately diverted to fill swimming pools. Or tourists can view a spectacular volcano from a distance by taking a helicopter flight over and around it. Working at tourist attractions is one way for people who live in volcanic regions to make a living.

On the edge

These tourists are looking into the crater of Volcan Poas in Costa Rica, which contains a mineral-rich lake.

From the air

A trip in a helicopter or light aircraft around a volcano is an exciting but safe way to watch an eruption at close range. People in this helicopter are watching an eruption of Mount Kilauea, a volcano in the Hawaii Volcanoes National Park.

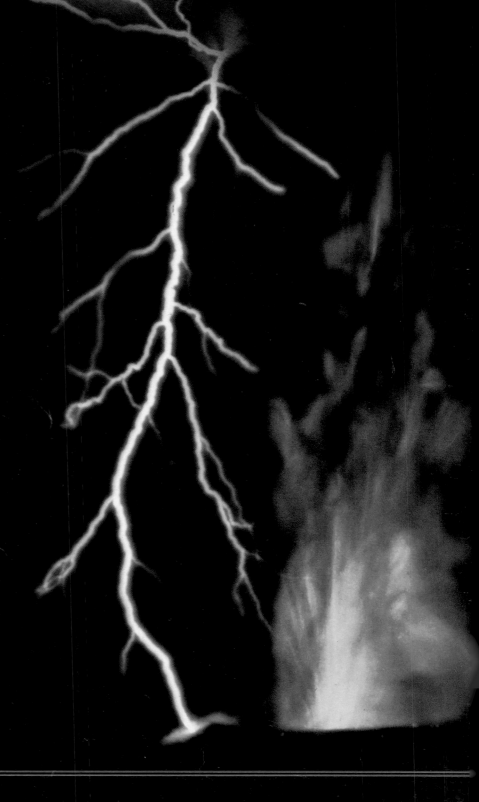

Lightning and fire
During an eruption,
a violent lightning
storm rages over the
summit of the Japanese
volcano Sakurajima.

Scream sunset
Edvard Munch's famous painting *The Scream*
is thought to show a volcanic sunset caused
by the eruption of Krakatau in Indonesia in
1883. The blood-red sunset could be seen as
far away as Norway, where Munch lived.

Volcanic weather

When Paricutin in Mexico was
erupting, from 1943 to 1952, not
a single person was killed by ash,
rocks, lava, gases, or mudflows.
But three people did die from being
struck by volcanic lightning. Many
volcanoes seem to create a massive
lightning storm directly above the
crater as they erupt. Scientists are
not sure why, but this could be caused
by ash, dust, or water particles that are
released from magma rubbing together
and building up an electrical charge.
This is just one of the ways in which
volcanoes can change the weather.

Red sky at night

Volcanic dust scattered through the atmosphere is sometimes called a volcanic haze. As well as creating red sunsets, a haze can give people breathing problems.

World weather effects

Volcanic lightning only happens very close to an erupting volcano, but other volcanic weather can affect a huge area—or even the whole planet. A really big eruption, such as that of Mount Saint Helens in 1980, throws so much ash and dust into the sky that it blocks out the sun over a large area, making day seem like night. As the dust spreads out and floats higher up into the atmosphere, it changes the way that the sun's light is scattered, leading to amazing bright red sunsets. Volcanic dust in the atmosphere also combines with water to make droplets of acid that absorb and reflect sunlight so that less heat and light reach Earth.

Global cooling

The eruption of Mount Tambora (above) in Indonesia in 1815 was the most violent explosive eruption in modern history, releasing four times as much energy as Krakatau. The ash and dust that it threw into the sky caused temperatures to drop around the world, and the following year, 1816, became known as "The Year Without a Summer."

STUDYING VOLCANOES

In 1991 volcanologists Katia and Maurice Krafft went to Japan to study and film an eruption of Mount Unzen. As they watched a pyroclastic flow surge down the mountain, the flow suddenly changed direction. The Kraffts, another volcanologist named Harry Glicken, and 40 journalists were killed. Working with volcanoes can be extremely dangerous, but volcanology is also exciting, adventurous, and very important.

Analyzing volcanoes

Like other scientists, volcanologists spend most of their time in laboratories. They analyze samples of lava, rocks, mud, and gases from volcanoes. They also study old layers of lava on volcanoes to try to find out when a volcano erupted in the past and when and how it could erupt again. Around one fifth of a volcanologist's time is spent visiting volcanoes to carry out fieldwork. This includes mapping old mudflows and lava flows, measuring changes in Earth that might predict an eruption, and, most daring of all, collecting hot lava, ash, and volcanic gases from erupting volcanoes.

Sulfur samples

This volcanologist is collecting sulfur deposits on the active volcano Mutnovsky in Kamchatka, Russia. Sulfur can form where sulfurous volcanic gases escape from craters and cracks on volcanoes.

Collecting lava

A scientist uses a special lava ladle to collect lava samples during an eruption of Kilauea in Hawaii.

Safety suit

Volcanologists sometimes have to work close to lava flows, where the heat is intense. A safety suit like the one shown below, covered in a silver coating, reflects heat away from the body and helps the scientist stay cool.

Predicting the future

Volcanologists can predict volcanic activity, which means that people who live close to a volcano can be warned of an eruption and escape in time. Luckily, most volcanoes give some warnings before a big eruption such as a series of smaller eruptions before the main one. Other signs are more difficult to see or hear, so volcanologists use special equipment to detect the changes that show that a big blast is on the way. They can also study a volcano's past, known as its "eruptive history," to find out when an eruption is likely to happen again.

Volcano observatory

When a volcano erupts constantly, volcanologists need to observe it all the time. Sometimes they build permanent observatories near volcanoes, where they can live full-time. This is the Montserrat Volcano Observatory, which monitors the Soufrière Hills volcano on the Caribbean island of Montserrat.

Measuring Earth

A geodimeter measures Earth's shape by sending out a laser beam that bounces off a receiver set up some distance away. By taking the same measurement many times, volcanologists can see if the time that the beam of light takes to bounce back is changing. If it is, this means that the distance is changing, and so Earth's shape is changing too.

Eruptions over time

The timeline below shows the eruptions of the dormant volcano Snaefellsjökull in Iceland. Volcanologists can calculate the history of a volcano from the layers of lava and ash around it. This may help predict the next eruption.

10000 B.C.   8460 B.C.   6050 B.C.   4550 B.C.

Eruption clues

There are several different clues that volcanologists use to predict eruptions. First, they study the shape of the ground; pressure from increased amounts of magma inside a volcano can make the ground bulge and crack. They use tiltmeters, which can detect the ground tilting, and geodimeters, which use lasers to sense changes in Earth's shape. Second, they measure how much gas a volcano is releasing. Volcanoes usually give off more gas just before an eruption as the magma inside pushes upward. Just like earthquakes, scientists use seismometers to pick up ground tremors—magma squeezing between solid rocks inside a volcano can make the ground shake.

Lava walking

Volcanologists often need to walk on or near freshly erupted lava as they explore active volcanoes. Sometimes a lava flow cools on the top but stays molten underneath, creating a solid "roof" that can support a person's weight.

Volcanology long ago

Volcanology is not a new science. The ancient Greeks and Romans studied volcanoes, and Italian scientist Lazzaro Spallanzani (1729–1799, below) made detailed studies of Mount Etna, measuring lava temperatures and analyzing volcanic gases.

4050 B.C.   2970 B.C.   2400 B.C.   2010 B.C.   1000 B.C.   A.D. 200

2270 B.C.

Today

Supervolcano!

What wiped out the dinosaurs? Some people say that it was an asteroid hitting Earth around 65 million years ago, throwing dust and debris into the atmosphere and blocking out the sun. Recently, however, some scientists have started to think that something else could have been responsible—a supervolcano. This is an enormous volcanic eruption, much bigger than any in recorded history. Studies of ancient lava flows show that these huge eruptions did happen in prehistoric times and could happen again. In a supervolcano, a vast magma chamber explodes out of the ground, releasing a lot more lava, ash, and rocks than the biggest eruptions of modern times.

Ready to blow

Yellowstone National Park in Wyoming sits on the site of an ancient supervolcano. It erupted around two million years ago, 1.3 million years ago, and 640,000 years ago. If it follows the same pattern, another eruption is due around now. The previous eruptions were so big that they covered most of what is now the U.S. in lava and ash.

Supervolcano size

A supervolcano would release at least 620 mi.^{3} (1,000km^3) of volcanic material—six times more than the biggest eruption in modern history. The biggest prehistoric supervolcanoes threw out as much as 620,000 mi.^{3} (1,000,000km^3) of rocks and other materials. Supervolcanoes do not form mountains. So much magma is blasted out of Earth that they leave bowl-shaped calderas. The edge of the huge caldera in Yellowstone National Park is easy to see today.

Dinosaur disaster

A supervolcano eruption could have killed the dinosaurs by filling the sky with dark ash and smoke. With sunlight unable to get through, plants would have died, and Earth's temperature would have dropped. Many animals would have run out of food. Others could have been killed by lava, poisonous gases, and pyroclastic flows.

ICELAND

Snaefellsjökull ● ● Laki
Eldfell ● Hekla
● Surtsey

● Novarupta (Alaska)

NORTH AMERICA

ATLANTIC OCEAN

● Rainier (Washington)
Saint Helens (Washington) ●
● Yellowstone (Wyoming)

PACIFIC OCEAN

HAWAII
● Mauna Loa
● Kilauea

● Paricutin (Mexico)
● Popacatépetl (Mexico)
Ilopango (El Salvador) ● ● Masaya (Nicaragua)
● Arenal (Costa Rica)
● Poas (Costa Rica)

● Soufrière Hills (Montserrat)
● Pelée (Martinique)

● Nevado del Ruiz (Colombia)
● Galeras (Colombia)

● Cotopaxi (Ecuador)

SOUTH AMERICA

World map of volcanoes

This map shows the world's best-known volcanoes, including all of the volcanoes mentioned in this book. You can see that many of them are found in the countries that lie around the Pacific Ocean. This circle of volcanoes is known as the Ring of Fire. Volcanoes are often found on small islands, where volcanic activity on the seabed has caused an island to form.

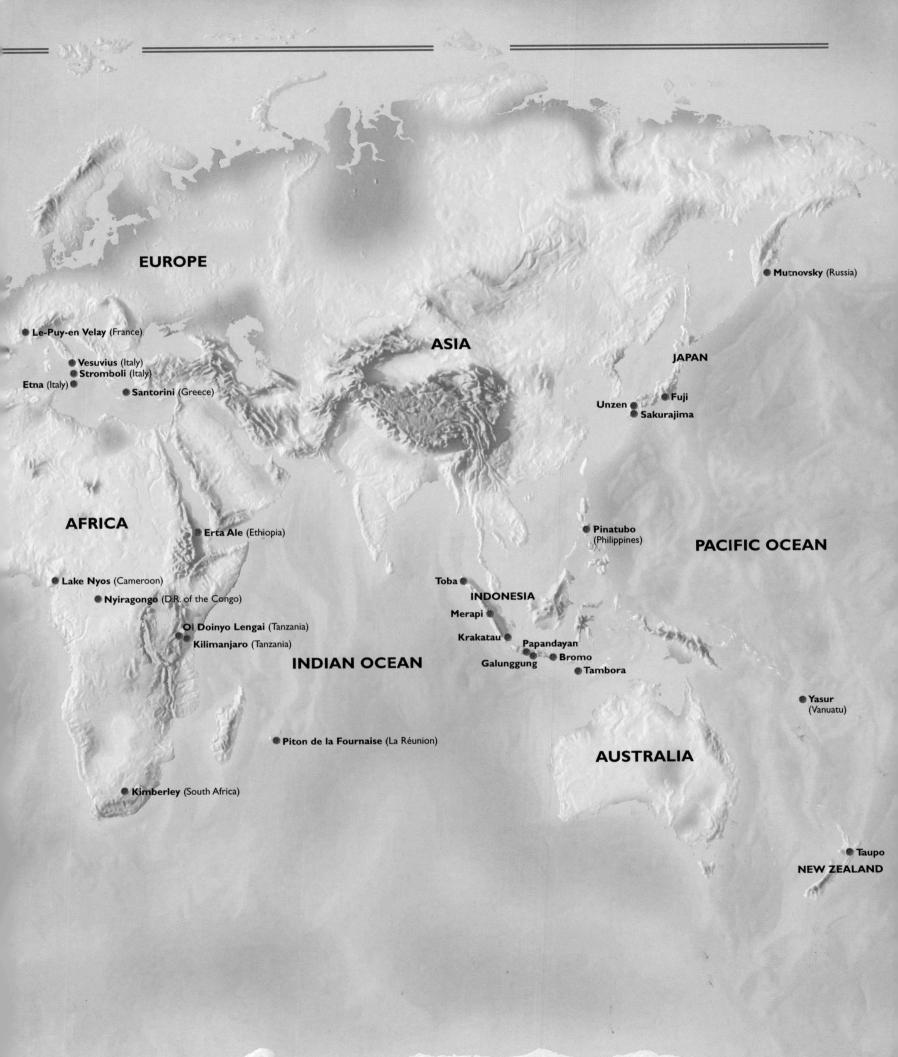

EUROPE

ASIA

JAPAN

● Mutnovsky (Russia)

● Le-Puy-en Velay (France)

● Vesuvius (Italy)
● Stromboli (Italy)
Etna (Italy) ●
● Santorini (Greece)

Unzen ● ● Fuji
● Sakurajima

AFRICA

● Erta Ale (Ethiopia)

● Lake Nyos (Cameroon)

● Nyiragongo (D.R. of the Congo)

● Ol Doinyo Lengai (Tanzania)
● Kilimanjaro (Tanzania)

● Pinatubo
(Philippines)

PACIFIC OCEAN

Toba ●

INDONESIA

Merapi ●

Krakatau ●
● Papandayan
Galunggung ● ● Bromo
● Tambora

INDIAN OCEAN

● Yasur
(Vanuatu)

● Piton de la Fournaise (La Réunion)

AUSTRALIA

● Kimberley (South Africa)

● Taupo

NEW ZEALAND

ERUPTION TIMELINE

This timeline lists some of the most famous and destructive volcanic eruptions and events ever known.

Date	Volcano	Description
c. 640000 B.C.	Yellowstone, U.S.	The most recent eruption of the supervolcano under what is now Yellowstone National Park covered most of North America with volcanic ash.
c. 70000 B.C.	Toba, Indonesia	The biggest volcanic eruption of the last two million years, this supervolcano released 1,740 mi.^{3} (2,800km^3) of volcanic material.
c. 1630 B.C.	Santorini, Greece	The Greek island of Santorini (also called Thera) was blown apart by a huge volcanic eruption, leaving a caldera. Thousands of people were probably killed.
A.D. 79	Vesuvius, Italy	Massive Plinian-type eruption destroyed the towns of Pompeii and Herculaneum with pyroclastic flows, killing at least 3,500 people.
1006	Mount Merapi, Indonesia	The major eruption devastated the island of Java, leading to the downfall of its ancient Hindu kingdom.
1631	Vesuvius, Italy	Another eruption of Vesuvius released lava and mudflows that claimed up to 3,500 lives.
1766	Hekla, Iceland	Iceland's biggest lava flow in history wiped out thousands of farm animals.
1772	Papandayan, Indonesia	The volcano collapsed in onto itself, releasing ash and debris that killed almost 3,000 people.
1783	Laki, Iceland	Lava flows and deadly gases destroyed farmland and livestock, leading to a famine that killed at least 9,000 people.
1792	Unzen, Japan	In Japan's worst-ever volcanic disaster, part of this volcano collapsed, causing a tsunami that killed up to 15,000 people.
1815	Tambora, Indonesia	The biggest, most violent eruption known in modern times. More than 90,000 people died in pyroclastic flows and then later from starvation and disease.
1822	Galunggung, Indonesia	Hot mudflows from this eruption claimed around 4,000 lives.
1883	Krakatau, Indonesia	Explosive eruption blasted the island of Krakatau to pieces, creating deadly tsunamis and turning skies red around the world. The death toll was around 36,000.

1902	Pelée, Martinique	A pyroclastic flow laden with burning gases from the erupting volcano enveloped the town of Saint Pierre, killing 28,000 people.
1919	Kelut, Indonesia	Hot mudflows from an eruption killed around 5,000 people.
1943	Paricutin, Mexico	A brand-new volcano grew from nothing after a crack appeared in a cornfield and began spewing out smoke, lava, and ash.
1951	Lamington, Papua New Guinea	Pyroclastic flows and choking dust from this volcano killed more than 3,000 people.
1963	Surtsey, Iceland	An underwater eruption broke through the water surface and created a new island.
1973	Eldfell, Iceland	This island eruption damaged the town of Vestmannaeyjar, but few people were hurt.
1980	Saint Helens, United States	A giant explosive eruption blew one side of the volcano away, and pyroclastic flows and ash falls flattened huge areas of forest. Fifty-seven people died.
1983	Kilauea, Hawaii	Kilauea began a long eruption that is continuing to this day.
1985	Nevado del Ruiz, Colombia	Around 23,000 people were killed when a massive mudflow formed during an eruption, swept down a river valley, and swamped the town of Armero.
1986	Lake Nyos, Cameroon	A huge cloud of carbon dioxide gas released from this volcanic lake suffocated more than 1,700 people to death in the village of Lower Nyos.
1989	Kilauea, Hawaii	Lava from Kilauea ruined a volcano tourist center and 45 homes in Hawaii.
1991	Pinatubo, Philippines	Warning systems and evacuations saved many thousands from this hugely violent eruption, although around 700 people were killed by mudflows and from homes collapsing under the weight of volcanic ash that fell on them.
1991	Unzen, Japan	During an eruption, a pyroclastic flow changed course and swept away 43 people, including three volcanologists.
1993	Galeras, Colombia	A sudden eruption took visiting scientists and tourists by surprise, killing nine people.
1997	Soufrière Hills, Montserrat	A large eruption killed 20 people and destroyed the island's airport.
2002	Nyiragongo, Democratic Republic of the Congo	Lava flows from this eruption killed only 45 people, but left 120,000 homeless.

FACTS AND RECORDS

The Volcanic Explosivity Index

A way of measuring a volcanic eruption, the Volcanic Explosivity Index (VEI) takes into account a number of different factors such as how violently the volcano explodes, how much volcanic material it throws out, how often it erupts, and how high its plume of smoke and ash rises up into the sky. The VEI, invented in 1982 by volcanologists Chris Newhall and Steve Self, has nine categories ranging from 0 to 8 (it can be extended to go higher if necessary). This chart shows how it works (all units are metric).

VEI	Description	Plume height	Volume of material	Eruption frequency	Volcano example
0	Nonexplosive	Up to 100m	$1,000m^3$	Daily	Kilauea
1	Gentle	100–1,000m	$10,000m^3$	Daily	Stromboli
2	Explosive	1–5km	$1,000,000m^3$	Weekly	Galeras, 1993
3	Severe	3–15km	$10,000,000m^3$	Yearly	Nevado del Ruiz, 1985
4	Cataclysmic	10–25km	$0.1km^3$	Every 10 years	Galunggung, 1822
5	Paroxysmal	More than 25km	$1km^3$	Every 50 years	Saint Helens, 1980
6	Colossal	More than 25km	$10km^3$	Every 100 years	Krakatau, 1883
7	Supercolossal	More than 25km	$100km^3$	Every 1,000 years	Tambora, 1815
8	Megacolossal	More than 25km	$1,000km^3$	Every 10,000 years	Toba, 70000 B.C.

The biggest eruptions

There were many massive and supervolcanic eruptions in prehistoric times, but we are not sure how big they all were, so this list shows the biggest volcanic eruptions in recorded history (in order of size). Volcanic eruptions are hard to measure, so different sources may give slightly different lists.

Volcano	Date	Km³ of material	VEI
Tambora, Indonesia	1815	150	7
Taupo, New Zealand	A.D. 181	100	7
Santorini, Greece	1630 B.C.	60	7
Krakatau, Indonesia	1883	25	6
Laki, Iceland	1783	25	6
Ilopango, El Salvador	A.D. 260	20	6
Novarupta, United States	1912	15	6
Pinatubo, Philippines	1991	10	6
Vesuvius, Italy	A.D. 79	3	5
Saint Helens, United States	1980	0.7	5

The deadliest eruptions

The deadliest volcanic eruptions ever are not always the same as the biggest eruptions, because the number of people that a volcano kills depends on how many people live close to it and how it erupts. Deadly volcanoes are the most famous volcanoes because they are the ones that make news stories. This list is in order of death toll.

Volcano	Date	Death toll	Deadly effects
Tambora, Indonesia	1815	90,000	Starvation
Krakatau, Indonesia	1883	36,000	Tsunamis
Pelée, Martinique	1902	28,000	Pyroclastic flows
Nevado del Ruiz, Colombia	1985	23,000	Mudflows
Unzen, Japan	1792	15,000	Tsunamis
Laki, Iceland	1783	9,000	Starvation
Kelut, Indonesia	1919	5,000	Mudflows
Galunggung, Indonesia	1822	4,000	Mudflows
Vesuvius, Italy	A.D. 79	3,500	Pyroclastic flows
Vesuvius, Italy	1631	3,500	Mud and lava

Most active volcanoes

The most active volcanoes in the world are those that erupt most often and produce the most lava and other volcanic materials. Scientists do not always agree on which volcanoes are the most active, and this list can change regularly.

Arenal, Costa Rica
Erta Ale, Ethiopia
Etna, Italy
Kilauea, Hawaii
Merapi, Indonesia
Ol Doinyo Lengai, Tanzania
Piton de la Fournaise, La Réunion
Stromboli, Italy
Unzen, Japan
Yasur, Vanuatu

Most volcanic countries

The countries listed below are among the most volcanic in the world, meaning that they have the most, biggest, and most active volcanoes. Each country is shown with a selection of its most famous volcanoes.

Country	Volcanoes
Colombia	Galeras; Nevado del Ruiz
Costa Rica	Arenal; Irazu; Poas
Iceland	Eldafell; Hekla; Laki
Indonesia	Krakatau; Merapi; Tambora
Italy	Etna; Stromboli; Vesuvius
Japan	Fuji; Unzen
Mexico	Paricutin; Popacatépetl
Philippines	Mayon; Pinatubo
U.S. (mainland)	Rainier; Saint Helens
U.S. (Hawaii)	Kilauea; Mauna Loa

Glossary

This glossary explains some of the words used
in this book and in other books about volcanoes.

aa A type of lava that cracks and
folds over as it cools, making rocks
with a rough surface.

active volcano A volcano that is
erupting or has erupted within the
last few hundred years.

archaeologist An expert who
studies old ruins and objects to find
out about past peoples and events.

ash Volcanic ash is made from lava
that cools and shatters as it is hurled
into the air.

ash plume The column of ash,
smoke, and dust that rises up into
the air from an erupting volcano.

block A lump of semimolten
lava that is thrown
through the air from
an erupting
volcano.

bomb A chunk of solid
rock thrown out of an erupting
volcano.

caldera A ring-shaped hollow
formed by a volcano collapsing.
Calderas are often filled with water.

cinder cone A volcano with
a triangular shape and a wide
crater, created by Strombolian-
type eruptions.

crater A wide, usually circular,
bowl-shaped opening at the top
of a volcano's vent, where lava
is thrown out of a volcano.

dike A smaller vent,
leading from the main
vent to the side of a volcano.

dormant volcano
A volcano that has not erupted
within the last few hundred years,
but could erupt again.

eruptive history The record of all
of the eruptions of a particular
volcano throughout its lifetime.

extinct volcano A volcano that has
stopped erupting and is not expected
to erupt again.

extrusive igneous rock Igneous
rock that forms when lava cools
after flowing out of a volcano onto
Earth's surface.

fertile Fertile soil is soil that
is rich and very good for
growing crops.

fieldwork Scientific study that
is done in the outside world—for
example, on an active volcano—
instead of in a laboratory.

fissure A crack in the ground where
volcanic gases or lava can escape.

flanks The slopes of a volcano.

fumarole A jet of steam that
escapes from a crack in the ground,
carrying volcanic gases along with it.

geodimeter A device that uses
lasers to detect changes in the shape
of the ground.

geothermal energy Heat energy
from inside Earth that can be used to
run power plants or heat homes.

geyser A jet of hot water and
steam that shoots out of the ground
periodically. Geysers are found in
volcanic areas where magma heats
underground water.

Hawaiian-type eruption A gentle
eruption in which runny lava flows
down the volcano's sides.

hot spot An isolated area of
hot, liquid magma under Earth's
crust that can create volcanoes
away from plate boundaries.

igneous rock Rock created when
magma or lava cools and hardens.

intrusive igneous rock Igneous
rock that forms when magma
cools underground inside a volcano
without reaching the surface.

lahar A river of mud that forms
when volcanic ash combines with
rain, melted ice, or river water.

lava Molten rock that flows out
of a volcano.

magma Molten rock inside Earth.

magma chamber A large area
underneath a volcano where magma
builds up before an eruption.

metamorphic rock
Rock that is created when
heat and pressure inside
a volcano change
existing rocks into
other types of rocks.

mudflow A river of mud that flows down the side of a volcano after an eruption. Also called a lahar.

observatory A building or station where scientists go to watch something such as the stars or a volcano.

pahoehoe A type of lava that cools to form smooth, ropelike rocks.

parasitic cone A mini volcano that forms where lava erupts out of a dike on the side of a volcano.

pillow lava Lava that cools underwater, forming pillow-shaped lumps.

pipe A tube carrying magma from a magma chamber up inside a volcano.

plate boundary An area where the edges of two or more tectonic plates meet and where most earthquakes and volcanoes are found.

Plinian-type eruption A violent, explosive eruption caused by a buildup of thick, sticky lava.

pyroclastic flow A fast-moving surge of rocks, gases, and volcanic ash released by some types of very violent volcanic eruptions.

seamount A mountain under the sea. Many seamounts are created by volcanic eruptions on the seabed.

seismometer A device that detects tremors and vibrations in Earth's crust.

shield volcano A volcano with a wide, flat shape, created by runny lava spreading out over a wide area.

spreading ridge A plate boundary where magma rises out of Earth between two tectonic plates, pushing them apart and creating new sections of Earth's crust.

stratovolcano A tall volcano with a pointed tip, created by explosive eruptions of sticky lava.

Strombolian-type eruption A volcanic eruption in which lumps of lava fly upward out of the volcano's crater.

subduction zone A plate boundary where one tectonic plate is pushed underneath another one.

supervolcano A very big volcanic eruption, bigger than any in recent history, that releases 621 mi.^{3} (1,000 km^3) or more of volcanic material.

tectonic plates The huge sections of rock that fit together to make up Earth's crust.

tephra Solid volcanic material ejected from an erupting volcano such as ash, rocks, and dust.

tiltmeter A device that can detect changes in the angle of the ground's surface.

tremor A shaking or vibrating of Earth that often occurs shortly before a volcano erupts.

tsunami A huge wave that can be caused by a volcanic eruption at or below sea level.

vent A tube carrying magma from inside a volcano to the surface, where it flows out as lava.

Volcanic Explosivity Index (VEI) A scale designed to measure and categorize volcanic eruptions by their size, violence, and frequency.

volcanic haze Dust and ash that collect in the atmosphere after a big volcanic eruption.

volcanic lightning Lightning that forms directly above an erupting volcano.

volcanic plug A tower of cooled, hardened lava from the inside of an ancient volcano that has mostly worn away.

volcanologist Someone who studies volcanoes.

volcanology The science of volcanoes.

Index

Further reading

Books

The Best Book of Volcanoes by Simon Adams, Kingfisher Publications, 2001

Volcanoes (Eyewitness series) by Susanna Van Rose and Ian Mercer, Natural History Museum, 1999

Violent Volcanoes (Horrible Geography series) by Anita Ganeri, Scholastic Hippo, 1999

Earthquakes and Volcanoes (Looking at Landscapes series) by Alison Rae, Evans Brothers Ltd., 2005

Websites

VolcanoWorld:
http://volcano.und.edu/

How Volcanoes Work:
www.geology.sdsu.edu/how_volcanoes_work

Global Volcanism Program:
www.volcano.si.edu/index.cfm

Supervolcano:
www.bbc.co.uk/sn/tvradio/programmes/supervolcano

Savage Earth volcano animation:
www.pbs.org/wnet/savageearth/animations/volcanoes

Acknowledgments

The publisher would like to thank the following for permission to reproduce their material. Every care has been taken to trace copyright holders. However, if there have been unintentional omissions or failure to trace copyright holders, we apologize and will, if informed, endeavor to make corrections in any future edition.

The publisher would like to thank the following for supplying photographs for this book:

b = bottom, *c* = center, *l* = left, *r* = right, *t* = top

4*tl*, 11*tr*, 11*cr*, 17*tr*, 30*tr*, 31*cr*, 49*tl*, 50*br*, 51*tr*: U. S. Geological Survey;
4*tr*: Yann Arthus-Bertrand/corbis;
5*c*: Mosista Pambudi/shutterstock;
6*tr*: Bychkov Kirill Alexandrovich/shutterstock;
6*b*: Douglas Peebles/corbis;
8–9*tc*: Roger Ressmeyer/corbis;
9*br*: Bembaron Jeremy/corbis sygma;
12–13*b*: Larry Dale Gordon/zefa/corbis;
13*tc*: Tashka/dreamstime.com;
14–15*b*: Anders Ryman/corbis;
15*tr*: NOAA (National Oceanic & Atmospheric Administration);
16–17*b*: Sergio Dorantes/corbis;
18–19*b*: Index Stock Imagery/photolibrary;
18*bl*: Bart Parren/shutterstock; 19*br*: Albo/shutterstock;
22–23*c*: Yann Arthus-Bertrand/corbis;
23*tr*: Colin Palmer Photography/alamy;
24–25*b*: Jacques Langevin/corbis sygma;
25*br*: Jacques Langevin/corbis sygma;
26*bl*: Michael Maslan Historic Photographs/corbis;
27*tr*: Wendy Kaveney Photography/shutterstock;
29*tr*: Rykoff Collection/corbis; 29*br*: Peter Turnley/corbis;
34–35*bl*: Science Photo Library/photolibrary;
35*tr*: Bob Krist/corbis; 36–37*bl*: Michael Almond/shutterstock;
38*tr*: Karl Kanal/istockphoto;
40–41*tc*: Craig Hansen/istockphoto;
40*bl*: Araldo de Luca/corbis;
42–43*bl*: Sigurgeir Jonasson, Frank Lane Picture Agency/corbis;
43*tl*: Iberto Garcia/corbis; 44*b*: David Watkins/shutterstock;
44*bl*: Hans Strand/corbis; 45*br*: Douglas Peebles/corbis;
45*tl*: Dave G. Houser/corbis; 46*br*: Phototake Inc/photolibrary;
46*tl*: Burstein Collection/corbis; 47*t*: Pacific Stock/photolibrary;
47*bl*, 48*bl*, 49*br*, 50*tr*: Science Photo Library/photolibrary;
53*tl*: Karel de Pauw/alamy